Days to Come

MANY**SEASONS**PRESS

Mesa, Arizona · 2022

Days to Come

and other poems

Paul Love

FIRST EDITION

Days to Come
And Other Poems

Copyright © 2022 Paul Love

MANY**SEASONS**PRESS

Published by Many Seasons Press
an Imprint of Multimedia Publishing Project
PO Box 50553
Mesa, Arizona 85208-0028
480-939-9689 | MultimediaPublishingProject.com

Book designed by Yolie Hernandez
(AZBookDesigner@icloud.com)

Paperback ISBN: 978-1-956203-11-0
eBook ISBN: 978-1-956203-13-4

Library of Congress Control Number: 2022945055

Printed in the United States of America.

To Mother and Dad
Never forgotten,
Always loved.

Contents

Days to Come

Through The Night

HOLD ME CLOSE AND WATCH MY EYES
For soon I will be gone.
Give me your love and all its warmth
You're mine until the dawn.

THE DAYS WILL PASS, OUR PATHS MAY CROSS
But things won't be the same.
I love you now but it can't last
So fragile is the flame.

TOUCH MY SOUL, I WANT YOUR FACE
Burnt deep into my mind.
So years from now I'll still recall
The night that you were mine.

AS I GROW OLD MY LIFE WILL CHANGE
But still I know, somehow,
I'll always dream of all the love
I'm feeling for you now.

I'LL LOVE AGAIN BUT THROUGH IT ALL
I'll hold your memory tight.
For years from now that's all I'll have
To get me through the night.

The Sea

SUN DRENCHED BEACHES AND TURQUOISE LAGOONS
Are places on Earth I have seen.
High soaring peaks, towering icebergs
And long, luscious shorelines of green.

TRANQUIL RED SUNSETS, WARM SUMMER DAYS
High flying birds on the wing.
Dark stormy nights, huge, crashing surf
Creatures that bite and can sting.

LOVERS HAVE WALKED AT NIGHT ON MY SHORES
Gazing at me hand in hand.
Feeling devotion, passion, and joy
Lying in love on the sand.

BRAVE MEN HAVE CROSSED ME, OTHERS HAVE FAILED

Now resting alone in the deep.

I've led some to freedom, others to chains

Led some to war, some to peace.

SAILORS AND SOLDIERS HAVE RIDDEN MY WAVES

Traveling on to the fight.

Saying a prayer to the heavens above

Hoping to live through the night.

ALL OF THESE STORIES, BEAUTIES, AND WONDERS

They have been given to me.

Still it remains, forever and always

Cold and alone, I'm the sea.

Our Place

I WALK BENEATH A SKY SO VAST
Along a trail where once we passed.
I live my days without you now
And though you're gone, your memory lasts.

THE CREEK STILL FLOWS, THE SONGBIRDS SING.
The flowers bloom with coming spring.
I stroll among the lofty trees
Where green moss grows and vines still cling.

THIS PLACE WAS OURS IN DAYS GONE BY
We'd dream and plan, the time would fly.
We'd make a wish for days ahead
And wait to hear the wind's reply.

WE HIKED OUR PATH A FINAL TIME
Now I'm not yours and you're not mine.
This land now means so much to me
Our special place is like a shrine.

I VISIT HERE TO FEEL YOU NEAR
I speak my heart but you don't hear.
I wish this spot could take me back
But it can't melt away the years.

Socorro

WEST LIES SOCORRO, THE PLACE OF MY DREAMS.
New Mexico's magic is endless it seems.
High on the banks of the great Rio Grande
Hot, blazing sun shines on cool, desert sands.

LAS CRUCES IS SOUTH, UP NORTH SANTA FE.
The river keeps flowing day after day.
To east and to west high mountains arise
Hawks soar above in blue, cloudless skies.

THE GIRL I'LL LOVE, SHE WAITS FOR ME THERE.
I know I will find her, this maiden so fair.
Then stay in Socorro for all of our life
I won't stop to rest until she's my wife.

IF SHE WILL HAVE ME, WE'LL BUILD OUR NEW HOME
On land that will give life and places to roam.
Our family will grow, our kids will be strong
Our lives will be happy, prosperous, and long.

WE'LL LIVE IN SOCORRO TILL OUR TIME IS GONE.
Finally, someday, we'll sing our last song.
Then lying forever on our precious land
Peaceful together beneath desert sands.

Morning Walk

EACH DAY STARTS WITH A BRISK STROLL.
It makes this old engine run.
Staying in shape is the goal
Aging is not so much fun.

THESE LEGS ARE STIFFER THAN LAST YEAR
First steps of my walk are slow.
My aches seem to have no cure
Where is that get up and go?

THE MORNING WALK'S A DELIGHT
My favorite part of the day.
Three miles feels about right
The legs are pumping away.

BIRDS AND WILDLIFE ARE WAKING
Venturing out from their rest.
The songs they sing are making
This part of the day the best.

PINK DAWN OVER THE MOUNTAIN
Looks down on the land so still.
Ice forms under the fountain
The breeze brings a morning chill.

SO MANY FRIENDLY NEIGHBORS
Say hi to me on the way.
All are pleasant and wavers
Brighten my morning do they.

MY MORNING WALK'S MY POTION
It treats whatever might ail
Keeps me always in motion
Works each day without fail.

Doc Holliday

BACK THROUGH THE MISTS OF TIME TO A WORLD FAR AWAY
You'll see a lonely rider, his name's Doc Holliday.
He started off in Georgia, studied dentistry,
He planned to live a quiet life, but that was not to be.

TROUBLE SEEMED TO FIND HIM, BUT HE
WOULD NOT BACK DOWN,
And when he killed his first man he headed out of town.
He moved out west to gamble, a gentleman of means,
He always stayed where lawmen were few and far between.

THE GAMBLERS NEVER CROSSED HIM,
THE ONES THAT DID GOT DEAD,
They knew that cheating Doc meant a bullet to the head.

His only girl was Big Nose Kate, a lady of the night,
They loved each other now and then,
but mostly they'd just fight.

DRIFTING ON TO TOMBSTONE, A NEW STOP IN HIS SEARCH,
He found his only friend there, the lawman, Wyatt Earp.
Doc thought he'd found a home there,
a place where he could stay,
But all of Tombstone's outlaws grew bolder every day.

THE OUTLAW GANG, THE COWBOYS,
KEPT SHOOTING UP THE TOWN,
It fell to Earp, the lawman, to take the Cowboys down.
The Cowboys made a challenge, a gunfight face to face,
The time would be tomorrow, OK Corral the place.

BUT EARP WAS NOT ALONE THERE, HIS BROTHERS AT HIS SIDE,
And Doc stood right there with them,
the outlaws could not hide.
Doc's scatter gun spoke quickly, spewing deadly lead,
The Earps were all still standing, the outlaws mostly dead.

THE COWBOYS ALL WERE BURIED BUT DOC WAS MOVING ON,

He mounted up to ride north, Tomb-

stone's dreams were gone.

Now Doc he was a lunger, his breathing getting bad,

He headed for the mountains, the only chance he had.

HE FOUND THE PLACE HE'D LOOKED FOR

WITH HEALTHY MOUNTAIN AIR,

Glenwood Springs was perfect, no more outlaws there.

But he didn't last much longer, he's buried now and yet

Doc Holliday is someone we never will forget.

Seven Seas Inn

SPRING HAD ARRIVED, IT WAS TIME TO BEGIN.
Dad and I set out on our trip as planned
To stay awhile at the Seven Seas Inn.

IT WAS SEVENTY-NINE, I WAS STILL YOUNG.
I was excited to spend time with Dad
Seeing the country and having some fun.

THE SEVEN SEAS INN WAS ON THE WEST COAST.
South of La Jolla is where we were aimed
We'd get there in three days, four at the most.

TWO THOUSAND MILES FROM BEGINNING TO END.
We talked and we joked, the hours flew by
Driving with Dad, my forever best friend.

FIRST THROUGH THE OZARKS, TALL HILLS OF GREEN.

On then to Texas, past canyons and bluffs

The sunsets there were like nothing I'd seen.

IN OKLAHOMA A TIRE WENT FLAT.

We got it repaired and kept rolling on

New Mexico's where we dodged a speed trap.

DESERTS IN YUMA, MOUNTAINS IN FLAGSTAFF.

The gas station boy showed us his pet frog,

Thirty years later, that still made us laugh.

THEN WE ARRIVED AT THE SEVEN SEAS INN.

A tasty buffet was all you could eat,

Saw Johnny Carson before we turned in.

THE NEXT SEVERAL DAYS WERE FUN IN THE SUN.

Golf at Torrey Pines and walks on the beach.

We'd seen the whole town before we were done.

SOMETIMES I STILL VISIT THAT OLD MOTEL.
Dad's gone now but still with me like then
With memories to share and stories to tell.

I WISH I COULD BE WITH MY DAD AGAIN
Sharing good times at the Seven Seas Inn.

Jewels and Gold

TIME IS MORE PRECIOUS THAN JEWELS AND GOLD.
It slips through your hands, it's so hard to hold.
Time is forever when you are a child.
The future is endless, days still to spend.
Time still for laughter, loving, and smiles
Time to be shared with family and friends.

TIME CAN'T BE BOUGHT NO MATTER YOUR NAME
No matter your riches, power, or fame.
We're given a gift, the days of our lives,
To do as we choose, to find our own way.
It's not known when, but the end will arrive,
We hope in a time and place far away.

TIME'S TO BE TREASURED, WASTE NOT A MINUTE.

Days aren't forever, there is a limit.

When you've grown older, time is more dear.

Stop to remember the days of your past.

Hold on to your loved ones while they are here,

And have your say now, the years will go fast.

Highway of Love

I'M BROKEN DOWN ON THE HIGHWAY OF LOVE.

You walked out the door without a goodbye

Left me with nothing, I just wanna die.

Nowhere to turn on the highway of love.

THE ROAD RAN FOREVER, OUR LOVE WAS STRONG.

Your smile was sweetness, bright like the sun.

We'd stay together, the deal was done.

The highway of love we drove all day long.

NOW I'M ALONE ON THE SIDE OF THE STREET.

You found someone new and made me feel small.

Your promise of love meant nothing at all.

My heart is broken, my misery complete.

MILE AFTER MILE THE WAY STRETCHES AHEAD.
The path seems too far now that you are gone.
Sadness just haunts me from dusk until dawn.
I'm feeling hurt since our love is dead.

FACING DESPAIR ON THE HIGHWAY OF LOVE.
A life without you means nothing to me.
I want you darling, but you set me free.
Traveling forlorn on the highway of love.

Your Love

YOUR BEAUTY'S LIKE A BREATH OF AIR.
A face that shines like rays of sun.
The softness of your luscious hair
Flowing as it lies undone.
And lips that are as full as this
Must be meant just for me to kiss.

YOUR TOUCH IS LIKE A FEATHER BED
So smooth and gentle on my skin.
Your fragrant scent, it fills my head
With dreams that cause my mind to spin.
Your eyes that shine are bright and clear
They mesmerize me so, my dear.

YOUR VOICE IS LIKE WHEN ANGELS SING.

You whisper softly like the breeze.

Your words are kind and flattering.

I need you near me if you please.

Your passion for me leaves me weak

My heart beats fast, it's hard to speak.

YOUR BODY'S WARM, A BURNING FLAME.

Your tight embrace is ecstasy.

I love to hear you say my name

And promise not to set me free.

Desire like ours that feels so strong

Is truth itself, it can't be wrong.

YOUR HEART IS TRUE LIKE MOONLIGHT'S BRIGHT.

Your love is real like smiles and tears.

I want you every day and night.

Please love me now and through the years.

I love you so it has to be,

You're here on earth to be with me.

Where You Are

I'D WALK FOR MILES THROUGH DESERT SANDS.
I'd scale the tops of mountains high
With aching legs and freezing hands
Climb heretofore unconquered lands
To hear once more your gentle sigh.

I'D SWIM THE OCEANS OF THE WORLD.
I'd sail my ship to distant shores
Before the wind with sails unfurled
Through seething storms, tossed and hurled
To hold you in my arms once more.

I'D FLY WITH BIRDS UP IN THE CLOUDS.
I'd soar into the sky above

Through lightning bright and thunder loud
To heights that should be unallowed
To have once more your precious love.

I'D TRAVEL TO THE MILKY WAY.
I'd rocket to a distant star
Moving on where no one's strayed
Across the heavens, come what may
To be once more right where you are.

Dream Girl

EACH NIGHT I LONG FOR SLEEP'S EMBRACE
TO TAKE ME TO A SPECIAL PLACE.
A place where you belong to me, we live as one for all to see.
I'm only joyful, so it seems when I'm
with you, girl of my dreams.
I need you near, girl of my dreams.

AS I DOZE OFF AGAIN TONIGHT, I'LL RIDE
AGAIN MY HAPPY FLIGHT.
I'll meet you somewhere in my mind and
leave my real-world woes behind.
We'll live in bliss until I wake, with-
out you girl my heart will break.
If you're not mine my heart will break.

WHEN I'M WITH YOU MY LIFE TASTES SWEET, THE
EARTHLY WORLD JUST CAN'T COMPETE.
I'd rather live this fantasy, why must we face reality?
Don't end this dream, I'm still not done
with loving you girl, you're the one.
I want you so girl, you're the one.

EACH DAY MY HEAD'S BENT OUT OF SHAPE
AS I WAIT FOR THE NIGHT'S ESCAPE.
I wish again to have you near to soothe
my soul and calm my fears.
You'll come to me when night descends,
we'll share a love that never ends.
My love for you it never ends.

I'LL CLIMB ONCE MORE INTO MY BED TO
FIND YOUR VISION IN MY HEAD.
My love for you it seems so real, it must
be true, these things I feel.
I'm happy as I take my rest and dream
of you girl, you're the best.
I love my dream girl, you're the best.

Voyageur

I AM A VOYAGEUR, I CARRY ALL I NEED UPON MY BACK.

I live a life of freedom, I live my life far from the beaten track.

Danger's lurking everywhere, it waits

for me at each and every turn.

But life seems so much sweeter here since

what I have is only what I've earned.

I'M MOVING WHEN THE MORNING BREAKS, AND THE

SUN WILL SET BEFORE THE DAY'S WORK'S DONE.

I fight against the winter snow, bat-

tle against the blazing summer sun.

Loneliness is by my side, staying with me till my travels end.

And yet I know I'm not alone, the run-

ning river treats me as a friend.

VOYAGEUR, OH VOYAGEUR, SINGING MY SONGS

AND TRAVELING ACROSS THE LAND.

Voyageur, oh voyageur, I sing my song as well as any man.

FROM MONTREAL TO GRAND PORTAGE, FROM

GRAND PORTAGE TO ATHABASCA LAKE.

It's a trip that takes a lot of courage, a lot of

strength, and a lot of sweat to make.

Minutes sometimes pass like hours, feet can of-

ten seem much more like miles.

But when my journey's over with, I know that

all I've done has been worthwhile.

Love Once More

YOU LOVED ME THROUGH THE SUMMER
My life was like a dream.
I felt the joy and wonder
From you, my own, my queen.

WE SLEPT TOGETHER DEEP IN LOVE
Our nights were endless bliss.
Our days were magic. Nothing could
Compare with your sweet kiss.

THE SUMMER LEAVES TURNED YELLOW
The chilly fall winds blew.
I knew my love was growing
But felt a change in you.

I TALKED ABOUT OUR FUTURE
The days ahead we'd spend.
But you were not so certain
You said our love might end.

YOU'RE LEAVING FOR THE WINTER
You have to clear your mind.
We might end up together
It just could take some time.

THE FALLING SNOW, IT TELLS ME
Of cold, dark days ahead.
And now I face the winter
Alone here in my bed.

FOR NOW YOU'LL KEEP ON SEARCHING
For things that make you free.
Choose between the life you want
And what can never be.

WE'LL FIND THE STRENGTH WITHIN US
To face what each day brings.
If everything works out all right
We'll love once more come spring.

Bluebird Day

FRESH FALLEN SNOWS UPON THE MOUNTAINS LAY.
Mornings now are cold, winter's here to stay.
Hawks fly up above searching for their prey.
All is clear and bright, it's a bluebird day.

EVERYTHING IS WHITE, COVERED NOW TILL SPRING.
All the trees are bare, leaves no longer cling.
Drifting snows are deep, gusting winds can sting.
There's a quiet peace only winter brings.

WATERFALLS ARE ICE, FROZEN STREAMS DON'T FLOW.
There's a small red fox, running on the go.
Pine trees standing tall, through their boughs winds blow.
High and cloudless skies shine on all below.

ON BLUEBIRD DAYS WHAT ONE MUST DO IS SKI.

I grab my boards and soon I'm flying free.

To make fresh tracks on powder days is key.

The first guy on the hill today is me.

THE MOUNTAIN IS MINE, THE RUNS ARE ENDLESS.

There aren't friends on powder days, I'm friendless.

Perfect snow, the skiing is tremendous.

A bluebird day like this is stupendous.

Always There

MY MOTHER WAS SPECIAL, BEYOND COMPARE.
Her love was endless, she'd be always there.
Be there to guide us wherever we were
Her time was for family, never for her.

WHEN I WAS LITTLE MY LIFE WAS SO FUN.
So much she taught me, new things to be done.
Each year on my birthday Mother would make
Homemade spaghetti and angel food cake.

HOCKEY AND BASEBALL WE'D PLAY IN THE YARD.
If I got sick it was board games and cards.
When summer came she'd drive us to the lake.
The joy it was endless, never a break.

AS TIME WENT BY I WAS MORE ON MY OWN
But she had my back, I wasn't alone.
For questions from class, the answers she'd know.
She knit me an afghan I treasure so.

THEN CAME THE DAY I MOVED WEST TO STAY
But my mother's love did not go away.
I had the support of Mother and Dad
Both in my corner with all that they had.

WE'D VISIT IN PHOENIX AND MICHIGAN
I never could wait to see them again.
Mother would cook meals and make welcome signs
It always was hard to leave them behind.

MOTHER'S TIME RAN OUT AT AGE NINETY-FIVE.
Her last year was sad with Dad not alive.
Our visits were precious in her last days
She was sweet and loving just like always.

NOW MOTHER IS GONE BUT NO DAY GOES BY
When I don't stop and look up to the sky
And think of her love and know that she cares.
For me, my mother will be always there.

Palo Verde

NO TREE DOES IT SEEM HAVE BRANCHES SO GREEN
As does Arizona's palo verde.
Its bark looks not white like aspens or birch might.
Its trunk it is narrow and sturdy.
Its branches are filled with more chlorophyll
To keep it alive through the seasons.
It grows where it's hot in deserts but not
In chilly or more rainy regions.

THIS TREE PROVIDES SHADE ON HOT SUMMER DAYS
It leafs out most during the monsoon.
Making cool spaces like an oasis
It's an escape on a hot afternoon.
Tucson and Phoenix are home to the green sticks

Translated from Spanish to English.
It has a mystique, appears so unique
As state tree it has been distinguished.

THESE TREES THEY ARE HOME TO CREATURES THAT ROAM
Cross the sands neath a blue desert sky.
This world is such that all of life must
Live by the code of the desert or die.
There among cacti, hot when the sun's high
The palo verde seeks out a living.
Too little water, life gives no quarter
The desert is so unforgiving.

Freedom

THE HIGHWAY'S FREEDOM, EVERY TURN
Excites my mind, my spirit yearns
To ride the road of no return.

A BRAND-NEW WORLD WAITS UP AHEAD.
It's time these chains of mine are shed.
I'll find a new life there instead.

THESE DETROIT WHEELS WILL GET ME THERE.
This ride has speed, more than its share.
It's got the guts and some to spare.

IT'S RUNNING HOT, THIS MUSCLE CAR.
My Dodge is built to travel far
Escape the city, *au revoir*.

THE ENGINE PURRS, THE TIRES WHINE.
It's rolling smooth between the lines.
This coupe performs, it's right on time.

THE BREEZE IS BLOWING THROUGH MY HAIR.
The music rocks, the speakers blare.
What's left behind I just don't care.

THIS BUGGY'S EATING UP THE ROAD.
I'm going to lighten up my load.
It's time I get the things I'm owed.

THE FREEWAY'S HEADING TOWARD THE SUN.
I guess I'll know when this ride's done.
I'll lose no more, it's time I won.

City Lights

HIGH ON A HILL ABOVE MY HOMETOWN
From my back porch I'm gazing down
Seeing the sights and hearing the sounds.
The scene is special come the late night
Watching the twinkling of city lights.

THE WORLD IS ASLEEP, ALL IS AT PEACE.
Little is heard, most traffic has ceased.
Mountains are seen faintly, off to the east.
Though little is stirring there down below
Always I see the city lights glow.

HERE I SIT ALONE, THE LIGHTS ARE A FRIEND.
I think of my day and where I have been.

I feel content and recharged again.

All seems to be right, my world aligns

As I sit and watch those lights softly shine.

THESE LIGHTS REMIND ME OF WHAT'S GONE BEFORE.

I find myself asking what's it all for?

Some memories I cherish, some I ignore.

People I've loved have sat here with me

Sharing the feeling of peaceful were we.

THE LIGHTS ALSO TELL ME WHAT LIES AHEAD

More life to be lived, more things to be said.

Don't waste any days, live them instead.

I'll be back here soon to gaze at this sight

And be once again with my city lights.

Autumn Chill

AN OLD MAN'S MOVING SLOWLY, WALKING DOWN THE STREET.
His coat is old and worn like the shoes upon his feet.
His mind recalls the friends and happy times he's known
But now he's all alone.

THE CITY SIDEWALK'S CROWDED BUT NO ONE KNOWS HIS NAME.
His days just run together, they're really all the same.
He'd like to find a friend, he still has love to share
But no one seems to care.

HIGH-RISE BUILDINGS REACH ABOVE STRETCHING TO THE SKY.
Inside the concrete gorges winds go whipping by.
Against the autumn chill the old man turns away.
Hard times are here to stay.

HIS LIFE WAS ONCE SO DIFFERENT, FILLED
WITH LOVE AND DREAMS.
Nothing was beyond him, the world was his it seemed.
But time went by so fast, the good years all were gone.
And still his life went on.

SO NOW HE ROAMS THE CITY, HIS DAYS ARE SAD AND COLD.
All of life is harder now that he's grown old.
He searches for some meaning, a reason still to live.
What has life still to give?

THE PEOPLE ALL ARE STRANGERS, CITY STREETS ARE MEAN.
No one's there to help him and dangers lurk unseen.
He thinks about his life and feels he's lost his way.
No hope for better days.

THE OLD MAN KEEPS ON GOING, FACING WHAT'S AHEAD.
Refusing to give up, he'll carry on instead.
He knows he's left with nothing but his strength of will
To face life's autumn chill.

Daredevil

HERE LIES THE CANYON DEEP.
Mist shrouds the cliffs so steep.
The river lies far below
Fast-running rapids flow.
Howling winds above are heard.
Hawks fly by, undeterred.

A ROPE RUNS RIM TO RIM
Made of steel, two inches thin.
A long stretch, wall to wall
A quarter mile in all.
The rope's high above ground
It's a thousand feet down.

THE TIGHTROPE MAN IS HERE.

His eyes they show no fear.

About to make his walk

It's glory that he stalks.

He takes a final breath

And starts his dance with death.

HIS FIRST STEP'S A SURE ONE

Much more work to be done.

Using all his talents

His pole gives him balance.

The daredevil moves fast.

Each step could be his last.

THE ROPE BEGINS TO SWAY

He's crouched but he's okay.

Now just a few steps more

He skips, his spirits soar.

At last he touches land

The walk has gone as planned.

AS KNEELING ON THE GROUND
And family gathers round
He bows his head to pray
In thanks for one more day.
His was an awesome feat
For now, his life tastes sweet.

Widow's Walk

THE SUN'S SLOWLY RISING UP FROM THE SEA.
The coastline's quiet, the town still asleep.
High up on a perch on top of the house
She stands facing east, her eyes gazing out.
She's made to herself a promise she'll keep.

THIS TURRET'S A HAVEN HIGH ON HER HOME
An open-air platform and red shingled dome.
The view is dramatic out to the bay
Waves crash on the shore exploding in spray.
It's her private place, she comes here alone.

SHE LEANS ON THE RAILING THERE AT HER POST
Daring to dream of the thing she wants most.

Her widow's walk is where she starts every day
A place she can hope, ponder, and pray.
She trusts what she seeks is more than a ghost.

HE CAME TO HER WORLD SOME YEARS AGO.
She loved him so much, more than he could know.
He felt the same and made her his wife.
Their union was perfect, sweethearts for life.
They lived for each other and watched their love grow.

THEN HE WENT TO SEA, IT'S BEEN NOW TWO YEARS.
He's not coming back she secretly fears.
But she won't give up, her faith is too strong.
For here in her arms is where he belongs
Holding her close and drying her tears.

SO SHE'LL KEEP TRYING TO SPEED UP THE CLOCK
Till his ship is back safe here at the dock.
Each morning will find her here at her spot
With each coming day she'll have the same thought
To see him once more from her widow's walk.

Forget You

YOU'VE BROKEN MY HEART, MY LIFE IT IS THROUGH.

I can't face the day, I lie here in bed.

The way that I feel I'm better off dead.

And everything's hopeless, I'm always blue.

We once were in love, oh yes, that is true.

Thoughts of your sweetness would fill up my head.

You made me happy with things that you said.

Now you just haunt me, I can't forget you.

YOU'VE FOUND A NEW LOVER, YOU WON'T SAY WHO.

One day you were mine, the next you were free.

You took all your things and dropped off the key.

I don't know what I am now supposed to do.

I'm living as one where once we were two.

I face life alone with no guarantees.

It's hard to believe this happened to me.

I know it will help if I forget you.

I GUESS I SHOULD TRY TO FIND SOMEONE NEW.

I must find a girl to heal my heart,

Someone to be kind, right from the start.

I hope if I love her, she'll love me too

And show me the world from a better view.

I'll find a new love if I'm to be smart.

I'll have to accept that we'll live apart.

For things to be right I must forget you.

Spirit Island

I CAN NO LONGER TAKE IT.
People are up in my face.
I'm not really sure what I'm going to do, but it's
Time to get out of this place.

DAYS ARE ALL SLOW AND BORING.
Life is no longer fun.
I waste all my time here spinning my wheels, and I
Guess it's best to be done.

IT'S TIME TO FOLLOW MY DREAMS.
Time to make it about me.
I can only guess what waits down the road, but I
Know for sure I'll be free.

I'LL GO FIND THE SUNSHINE.
I'll hang out on a beach.
I'll find some new friends to turn me around, and I'll
Learn whatever they teach.

I'VE FOUND MY NEW HEAVEN.
Spirit Island is its name.
My life will be different, not like before, and I'm
Sure I'll be glad that I came.

THIS ISLAND IS SPECIAL.
Life is lived without rules.
I doubt I will miss my old world and friends, I'm glad
To be rid of the fools.

I'LL SLEEP LATE IN THE MORNING.
Maybe I'll go for a swim.
I'll probably spend the afternoon drinking, that's
Better than going to the gym.

THIS PLACE MAKES ME HAPPY.
I feel no need to roam.
I bet I could never find someplace better, so
Spirit Island's my home.

Star In The Night

LONG PAST SUNDOWN WHEN ALL IS DARK
I can see my star in the night
Shining so bright.

IT SITS UP HIGH, NORTH OF THE MOON
Lighting the sky from its lofty perch
Guiding my search.

MY STAR HAS ALWAYS BEEN SPECIAL
It gave me strength and calmed my fears
Through all the years.

I FIRST SAW MY STAR WHEN I WAS YOUNG
And though now I'm over the hill
It's with me still.

MY STAR'S MY GUIDE, SHOWING THE WAY
It keeps me true, always on course
It is my source.

MY STAR GIVES LIGHT TO THOSE CLOSE TO ME
Shining down on those that I love
From high above.

THOSE WHO HAVE LEFT, GONE FROM MY LIFE
Must gaze at this star just like I do
They see it too.

ONCE MORE TONIGHT WHEN MIDNIGHT COMES
I'll find my star sparkling up high
There in the sky.

Gone So Soon

OUR DREAMS AND OUR MEMORIES MAKE OUR LIVES SWEET.
We relive our glories and wish on the moon.
Our past and our future make us complete.
With no dreams to strive for we feel out of tune
But dreams once achieved are all gone so soon.

GOOD TIMES AWAIT IN DAYS YET TO COME.
Much thought is given to how life will be
Where we are going and where we are from
Dreaming of people and places we'll see.
Life gives us hope but no guarantees.

OUR JOURNEY BEGINS, WE STRIVE FOR A GOAL.
A vision is seen of our future life

Something that thrills us and touches our soul
Someone to share with, a husband or wife.
Nights that are peaceful and days without strife.

IF WE ARE LUCKY OUR WISHES COME TRUE.
But goals once accomplished don't always last.
Life quickly will tarnish what once was new.
We find ourselves missing days that have passed.
But those times have left, the die has been cast.

YES, MEMORIES AND DREAMS CAN BRING US SUCH BLISS
Though daily affairs should not be impugned.
Hold on to your memories, do reminisce.
Dream as big as you can, nothing's immune.
Cherish your days, they'll be gone too soon.

Dance In The Rain

WHERE HAVE YOU GONE? WHAT HAVE YOU DONE?

Where is your love that I miss?

You were my girl, you were the one.

I lived for the taste of your lips.

Just when I thought our life had begun

You disappeared in the mist.

WHEN FIRST WE MET YOU WERE SO SWEET

I dreamed of you morning and night.

I held you close to feel your heat.

Your face was a beautiful sight.

I knew my life would be incomplete

Until I made you my wife.

MY LOVE FOR YOU WAS HARD TO EXPLAIN.
My feelings for you ran so deep.
Once I watched you dance in the rain.
I held you each night while you'd sleep.
Each day was a chance to love you again.
You gave me your heart for to keep.

HOW COULD IT HAPPEN? HOW COULD IT END?
Why are you not by my side?
Was our love real or was it pretend?
Shouldn't I be with my bride?
Us being apart I can't comprehend.
It would have worked if we tried.

SOMETHING IN YOU I DON'T UNDERSTAND.
How could you leave me alone?
I want it back, the life that we planned.
I don't want to be on my own.
I want you here holding my hand
Lost in the love we have known.

Sometimes

I WISH I COULD STAY HERE WITH YOU ONE MORE DAY
But the highway is calling to me.
There's someplace that I have to be.
I guess we could try to work it all out
But I know we'd just disagree.

I PROMISED TO HAVE AND HOLD YOU FOR LIFE
But I think it's time to resign.
I'm sure I'm just wasting my time.
Your understanding of how we should live
Is so much different than mine.

THERE'S A WHOLE NEW WORLD AND HAPPIER LIFE
Waiting outside the front door.

I just can't take anymore.
I know we were once so deeply in love
But it doesn't feel like before.

EVEN THOUGH YOU COULD HAVE TRIED HARDER
I want you to know it's all right.
I'll soon be out of your sight.
I can't put my finger on why it went wrong
Or why we always would fight.

YOU SHOULD GO AND GET ON WITH YOUR LIFE
Probably you'll find someone new.
Whatever we had is through.
Don't think about me or times that we shared
Or things that we used to do.

TONIGHT I'LL BE GONE AND OUT ON MY OWN SINCE
All the good times have been had.
I really doubt you'll be sad.
I won't be back but I'll always remember
That sometimes things weren't too bad.

Daydreams

BRIGHT MORNING GLARE, SALTY SEA AIR,
LONG STRETCH OF EMPTY BEACH.
Moon sits high, up in the sky, still faintly shining.
Hand in hand, on the sand, walking on the shore.
Cloudless blue skies, warm sun, big waves, and daydreams.

TIDAL POOLS, THE WATER COOL, DOLPHINS ARE SEEN PLAYING.
Rocky cliffs and nature's gifts rise up all around.
Sea crabs crawl, wind gently calls,
pine trees cling to the bluffs.
Cloudless blue skies, warm sun, big waves, and daydreams.

WALKING SLOW, PUTTING A TOE INTO THE SURGING SURF.
The sea is cold, uncontrolled, rushing onto the land.

Then turns about, sucking back out, rolling off to the depths.
Cloudless blue skies, warm sun, big waves, and daydreams.

Hand on my waist, beautiful face laughing and looking at me.
Time stands still, this day will last in my mind forever.
Just one kiss to seal this joy that we share today.
Cloudless blue skies, warm sun, big waves, and daydreams.

Your Ghost

YOU LEFT MY LIFE AND LEFT THIS TOWN.
There's little doubt you're gone for good.
Yet now it seems you're still around.
You haunt my mind more than you should.
Your ghost is here to hunt me down.

I SEE YOUR GHOST WHERE FIRST WE MET
Inside the park one day in spring.
Your presence there it lingers yet.
Within my head your memory clings.
The way you looked I can't forget.

WE SAW A FILM ON OUR FIRST DATE.
Your spirit seems to live there still

In the theatre your ghost awaits.
I feel a damp and eerie chill.
My mind is in an altered state.

YOUR GHOST HAS FOUND A PLACE TO STAY
Inside the house that once we shared.
I've made the choice to move away
Down the street where I'm not scared.
I only want to feel okay.

I WATCHED YOU WAVING FROM THE STREET
The day you said goodbye for good.
Now every day your ghost repeats
That final scene from where you stood.
There is nowhere I can retreat.

Trophy Boyfriend

I STAY IN BED TILL NOON OR ONE.
With my first beer my day's begun.
My plans today add up to none.
Anyone can see my girl's proud of me
Yes, I am a trophy boyfriend.

I'M HEADED FOR MY FAVORITE CHAIR.
Flip on the tube, I'll sit and stare.
A wasted day? I just don't care.
I highly doubt I'll leave the house.
Oh, I am a trophy boyfriend.

YES, I'VE BEEN CALLED A LAZY SLOB.
I guess it's true I have no job.

At least I'm not a haughty snob.
I don't do my share, my girl doesn't care
Since I am a trophy boyfriend.

MY GIRL SHE NEEDS SOME OVERTIME.
The money's low, the bills behind.
My contribution: not a dime.
She cleans every day and cooks when I say.
She knows I'm a trophy boyfriend.

MY GIRLFRIEND LOVES ME, SO I GUESS.
Our partnership's a real success.
She does a lot and I do less.
She'll never leave, we both believe
That I am a trophy boyfriend.

No Fear

I'VE BEEN IN A RUT.
New doors are shut.
Can't seem to find the why
Or what.

LEARNING HOW TO COPE.
Left with scant hope.
I'm nearing the end of
My rope.

RUNNING FROM THE PAST.
Time's going fast.
Knowing that the good years
Won't last.

WHAT SEEMED RIGHT IS WRONG.

I don't belong.

The odds of winning now

Are long.

THERE'S A BETTER WAY.

I've gone astray.

I want to be back in

The fray.

I STILL HAVE SOME TIME

To claim what's mine.

Even though I'm well past

My prime.

YESTERDAY IS DEAD.

That book's been read.

Time to face tomorrow

Instead.

THE NEW ME HAS BEGUN

What's gone is done.

It's time I actually had

Some fun.

I'M MOVING AHEAD.

My wings are spread.

I'm going to change just like

I said.

THE FUTURE IS CLEAR.

This is the year.

I'll live each new day with

No fear.

She Waits

SHE HAD A FRIENDLY FACE I COULDN'T SEEM TO PLACE
The day when first we met.
I'd seen her not before as she sat near my door
Just waiting for a friend.

HER FRIEND LIVED DOWN THE HALL BUT I COULD NOT RECALL
That we'd been introduced.
The friend was running late, I told her she could wait
Here in my room with me.

SHE THANKED ME AND SAID YES, SHE COULD NOT REALLY GUESS
Just when her friend would show.
We both went on inside my room where she'd decide
What she was going to do.

I HAD HER TAKE A SEAT, SHE TOLD ME I WAS SWEET
For letting her come in.
She had a certain charm and I could see no harm
In spending time with her.

SHE SEEMED TO LIKE ME TOO AND I THINK WE BOTH KNEW
Her friend was on her own.
I poured us both a drink and I began to think
This was a special day.

I SAT THERE NEXT TO HER AND SOMETHING IN ME STIRRED
I had not felt before.
We talked for hours on end, I asked if she would spend
The night alone with me.

SHE TOLD ME THAT SHE WOULD AND I KNEW THAT THIS COULD
Be special like a dream.
She hugged and held me tight and told me that tonight
I never would forget.

I SAID I'D PLAY A SONG IF SHE WOULD SING ALONG
With my six-string guitar.
We sang till we were hoarse but very soon of course
We ended up in bed.

WE GOT BENEATH THE SHEETS, SHE GENTLY RUBBED MY FEET

Till sleep had found us both.

By dawn I woke to see her sleeping so at peace

While lying next to me.

SHE WOKE AND SAID ALTHOUGH SHE REALLY HAD TO GO

She did not want to leave.

I said I understood but wouldn't it be good

If we could meet again.

I PLAYED HER ONE MORE TUNE, SHE

SAID SHE'D STOP BACK SOON

When she could find the time.

She gave me a last kiss on which to reminisce

Till I saw her again.

BUT THAT DAY HAS NOT COME, I GUESS OUR TIME WAS DONE

When she walked out my door.

My time with her was brief but it's still my belief

She waits for me somewhere.

Just One Chance

OUR DAYS ARE LIVED, THE TIME FLIES BY.
You get a ticket to the dance.
Be sure to make the most of it.
We only have but just one chance.

A CHANCE TO THANK THE ONES WE LOVE
For all the things that they have done.
A chance to find someone to hold
To share your life and live as one.

A CHANCE TO ALWAYS DO YOUR BEST
At anything that you might try.
To always make your move right now
Before that moment's passed you by.

A CHANCE TO SEE THE OCEAN WAVES
Breaking on the western shore.
Travel to a distant land
Someplace you've never been before.

A CHANCE TO LAUGH UNTIL IT HURTS
While staying up all night with friends.
Seek out someone you may have wronged
To clear the air and make amends.

LOOK FOR THE THINGS THAT GIVE YOU PEACE.
Try to improve your circumstance.
Squeeze every drop out of your life
And make the best of your one chance.

Across The Atlantic

NORTH ATLANTIC SKIES, DANGEROUS AND WINDY
Proved no match for the great Lucky Lindy.
Only Charles Lindbergh was up to the test.
His flight 'cross the ocean outdid the rest.

BORN IN DETROIT IN NINETEEN 0-TWO.
He learned to fly young, his skills quickly grew.
"Daredevil Lindbergh" performed flying stunts,
Then flew on a mail route for a few months.

BUT LINDY HAD THOUGHTS TO DO SOMETHING GRAND.
To fly shore to shore was what he had planned.
A trip that many already had tried.
None of them made it and most of them died.

HE ORDERED A PLANE THAT COULD MAKE THE TRIP.
Spirit of St Louis would be his airship.
This single-seat craft of his own design
Was just what he'd need to get there on time.

NEW YORK TO PARIS, THE TRIP WAS NONSTOP.
Thirty-three hours, he flew round the clock.
From storms, wind and fog there wasn't a break.
It was a challenge to just stay awake.

THOUSANDS AWAITED FOR HIM TO TOUCH DOWN.
His now was a life of world renown.
Three thousand miles from New York he'd flown.
How this changed his life he couldn't have known.

FIRST OVER THE OCEAN FROM WEST TO EAST
At age twenty-five a gigantic feat.
He conquered the world with his daunting flight.
Charles Lindbergh's star will always shine bright.

Love Meant To Be

THE SUN WILL ALWAYS RISE, THE BIRDS WILL SURELY SING.
I'll still be in love with you.
It's the way that you hold me, your sweet scent, and
All of the things that you do.

WHEN I LIE AWAKE, COLD AND ALONE IN MY BED
You come to me in the night.
You kiss and caress me with your gentle touch, and
Soon everything is alright.

SOMETIMES IF I HAVE A BAD CASE OF THE BLUES
I'll hear you knock at my door.
Then you come inside with smiles and laughter, and
I can feel good like before.

IF I'M FEELING HUNGRY YOU'RE THERE IN MY KITCHEN
To feed me lobster and wine.
You softly massage my sore, aching body.
Your touch is truly divine.

THE WAY THAT YOU LOVE ME AND MAKE ME SO HAPPY
Gives you the key to my heart.
It's hard to imagine that I could move onward
If we were ever to part.

MY ONE TRUE DESIRE IS THAT I GIVE TO YOU
The joy that you give to me.
Till the end of time and no matter what happens
Ours is a love meant to be.

Desert In Spring

DESERT BEAUTY BRINGS
More than anything
A special magic when it blooms
Every year come spring.

BENEATH LATE MARCH SUN
Summer's not begun.
All the world's in a soft glow
Until each day's done.

HIKING IS A TREAT
Biking on the streets.
Enjoying all the last cool days
Before summer's heat.

FLOWERS ARE IN BLOOM
Cacti will be soon.
Their lovely scent is heavenly
Each spring until June.

HUMMINGBIRDS HOVER.
Snakes soon discover
It's time to slither out from their
Warm, winter cover.

THESE DAYS ARE SUPREME.
The world is serene.
The blooming desert in springtime
Is just like a dream.

Love You Still

YOU SAID YOU LOVED ME LONG AGO
But when you left how could I know
That thoughts of you would hurt me so.
And yet I love you still.

I GUESS I REALLY CAN'T EXPLAIN
The way I just look past the pain
And hurt you caused that still remains.
I want you more each day.

THE WAY YOU'D HOLD ME IN THE NIGHT
Your soft caress at dawn's first light
You always made the world seem right.
I need that back again.

ANOTHER MAN IS WITH YOU NOW
And I get through my days somehow.
I look for love as time allows
But all I want is you.

I CALLED YOU UP ONCE ON THE PHONE
You couldn't talk, you weren't alone.
It seemed all wrong, I should have known.
But hearing you felt good.

THE LOVE WE SHARED IS WHAT I LACK.
I wish that you would take me back.
I cannot get my life on track
Unless you love me too.

Porch Swing

HER PORCH SWING'S BEEN A FRIEND.

From day one till the end.

A place she's gone to rest and think of happy times.

She's had a happy life.

It all has worked out right.

Her porch swing's shared with her

these moments so sublime.

UPON HER WEDDING DAY

She heard her husband say

While sitting on their swing, he'd love her evermore.

Their love was oh so sweet

Her happiness complete.

She knew a life of joy was what they had in store.

HER BABIES NUMBERED THREE

She'd rock them all to sleep.

There swinging on her porch, daylight would fade away.

The kids would laugh and sing

When older they would swing

While eating chocolate ice cream on a summer's day.

EACH DAY SHE'D WORK SO HARD

Indoors and in the yard

And when she'd need to rest, her porch swing was the place.

Her friends would come to call

She grew to love them all

Her swing it was the spot they'd visit face to face.

THE YEARS HAVE QUICKLY PASSED

The kids grew up so fast.

She feels the lasting bliss of life with no regrets.

Her husband takes her hand

And they both understand

Sharing their old porch swing is as good as it gets.

Sixty-Five

MANY LONG YEARS FROM NOW
I'll stop and think of how
It felt to be alive
When I was sixty-five.

ALL TOO SOON I'LL BE OLD.
It comes fast I've been told.
But until that arrives
I'll enjoy sixty-five.

I CAN STILL RACE MY BIKE
Have a swim, take a hike.
On most days there's no pain.
I remain mostly sane.

EYES AND EARS WORK OKAY.
Yes, the hair's all gone gray.
I can still have some fun.
No, this ride's far from done.

MY SWEET GIRL TREATS ME RIGHT
All the time, day and night.
Our love's real, our love's true
Never dull, always new.

MY FAMILY'S IN MY HEART.
They've been there from the start.
They've always had my back
An undisputed fact.

MY FRIENDS THEY MEAN SO MUCH
We're never out of touch.
I'm lucky to have known
These friends I call my own.

MY DAYS ARE GOOD INDEED.
I have all that I need.
The world's a lovely place
I truly can embrace.

THE LIFE I HAVE TODAY
Will fade along the way.
This world where I belong
Will someday all be gone.

BUT I CAN LIVE IT NOW
As long as time allows.
I will not be deprived
Of life at sixty-five.

My Michigan Home

I'VE SEEN OUR COUNTRY AND TRAVELED THE GLOBE.
Always a drifter and thirsting to roam.
But no matter where my wanderings have led
I've always returned to my Michigan home.

MY ROOTS RUN SO DEEP IN MICHIGAN SOIL
Where loved ones were born and some laid to rest.
Memories were made there and life lessons learned.
It's offered me more than I could have guessed.

I LOVE TO GO BACK AND GAZE AT SIGHTS LIKE
Manitou Island and Grand Traverse Bay.
Nothing feels better than taking a swim
In chilly Burt Lake on hot summer days.

DETROIT IS THE HOME OF AUTOMOBILES
And Lansing is where the Capital's found.
Holland is known for tulips in springtime.
I've always had fun in Grand Rapids town.

THE MACKINAC BRIDGE GOES OVER THE STRAITS
For those traveling north up to the U. P.
The massive Great Lakes encompass the land.
The Soo Locks reside in Sault Ste Marie.

SKIING IN WINTER IS GREAT UP IN BOYNE.
Golf courses abound like gorgeous Gull Lake.
The Pistons and Lions, Tigers and Red Wings
Will show you no mercy, make no mistake.

IF I'VE BEEN GONE FROM MY STATE FOR TOO LONG
It calls to me if I stop and listen.
Though I've journeyed far, no feeling compares
With going back home to my Michigan.

Come With Me

WON'T YOU COME WITH ME
To share my life and be my wife?
Please say you will stay
And you'll be mine till end of time.

TELL ME YOU WON'T GO.
You need to be right here with me.
Let's begin today.
It feels so right, you'll see the light.

I CAN'T LIVE ALONE
Without you here. Don't disappear.
Say that you love me.
Make me rejoice to hear your voice.

LET ME GIVE YOU LOVE.

Take my hand, you'll understand.

Don't you be afraid.

I need you so, let yourself go.

I'LL MAKE YOU HAPPY.

You will smile all the while.

Lonely days are gone.

Our love is true, you won't be blue.

IF YOU WALK AWAY

I know you'll make a big mistake.

You belong with me.

The world is ours, it's in the stars.

TELL ME YES RIGHT NOW.

Do not delay another day.

I know you're scared

But saying no would hurt me so.

JUST SAY YOU'LL BE MINE.

You have to choose, what's there to lose?

Give this a chance.

You'll have my heart right from the start.

I WILL BE SO GLAD

If you decide to take this ride.

Happy evermore

If you agree to come with me.

Still In Mississippi

YOU'RE STILL IN MISSISSIPPI

While I watch the sunset from our mountain home

Facing life here all alone.

Without you beside me I cannot be free.

IT'S SIX MONTHS SINCE YOU LEFT ME.

It wasn't me you said, you just needed some space.

Some choices you had to face.

You felt it was best though I did not agree.

YOU'VE STARTED A NEW LIFE THERE.

The man who lives next door, you mentioned him again.

You said he's just a friend.

Just someone to hang with, not a love affair.

YOU SEEM TO HAVE A NEW HOME.

Please tell me what you've found in Mississippi.

You need to make me see.

I don't think you love me, I guess I should have known.

I WISH SOMETIMES YOU'D CALL.

You said you're busy and I need to understand.

You'll touch base when you can.

I feel the day may come when you won't call at all.

How did this come to be

With us so far apart and ending up this way?

But I know you will stay

Far from where we were, there still in Mississippi.

Solitude's Sound

IN THE QUIET OUTSIDE TOWN
You can hear solitude's sound.
Nature's voice is all around.
Songs of peace and joy abound.

THE BABBLING CREEK GENTLY FLOWS
Carrying melted winter snow
Gurgling downstream as it goes
To thirsty ground far below.

BIRDS ARE CALLING HIGH ABOVE.
Hear the haunting mourning dove.
Robins chirping words of love
And owls hooting just because.

COYOTES HOWLING IN THE NIGHT
Coming out with dusk's last light
Staying stealthy, out of sight.
Their prey is wide awake with fright.

WIND BLOWS GENTLY THROUGH THE TREES
Moving boughs with rustling leaves.
Sounds move lightly on the breeze
Putting mind and soul at ease.

SOLITUDE'S SOUND IS NATURE'S CURE
Softly drifting to your ears.
Worries quickly disappear
With the music that you hear.

Think Of Me

WHEN YOU WAKE UP ALONE
In bed with just your phone
I hope sometimes you think of me
And good times we have known.

IF SKIES ARE DARK AND GRAY
When you begin your day
I hope my memory turns skies blue
As you start on your way.

SOME DAYS YOUR JOB IS ROUGH.
Your best is not enough.
I wish that if I crossed your mind
Work might not seem so tough.

WHILE YOU'RE OUT ON THE TOWN
With strangers all around
I wonder if you stop and think
Of where I might be found.

AS YOU TURN OUT YOUR LIGHT
To face another night
I pray that you would wish me there
To make it all seem right.

IT SOMETIMES SEEMS TO BE
You just want to be free.
But I think of you all the time.
I hope you think of me.

Now I'm Lost

MY LOVE FOR YOU CAME WITH A COST.

I once was found but now I'm lost.

I can't find my way.

You touched my heart and made me feel

As though our love was truly real.

But now our love is gone to stay.

I HOPED THAT YOU WOULD BE MY GIRL.

You brought me peace and changed my world.

Happiness was mine.

I still can taste your sweet first kiss.

I fell into love's deep abyss.

Your touch was soft and you were kind.

IT'S STRANGE HOW LOVE JUST DISAPPEARS
As if by magic, smoke, and mirrors.
Oh where does it go?
One night you're holding me in bed.
When morning comes our love is dead.
What lies ahead we just can't know.

I HAD YOUR LOVE AND LOST IT ALL.
I risked my heart and took the fall.
Into the dark I've crossed.
Where once my life looked bright and new
It's shaded now with grays and blues.
I once was found but now I'm lost.

Days To Come

I USED TO DREAM OF FUTURE PLANS
Of things to do before I die.
But time has slipped right through my hands.
The days to come have all gone by.

I THINK OF DAYS OF YOUTH NOW GONE.
I think of people I have known.
Those days have passed but life goes on
Sometimes I find myself alone.

THERE ARE SOME THINGS I'D LIKE TO CHANGE
Some things I wish that I had said.
The past cannot be rearranged.
I have to face what lies ahead.

MY LIFE IS GOOD, I STILL AM BLESSED
With many gifts that make me smile.
But if I could, I would request
To relive old times for awhile.

I'M GLAD MY LIFE'S BEEN FILLED WITH CHEER.
Tomorrow's looming round the bend.
I'll have to deal with each new year.
Old times aren't coming back again.

IF I COULD TRAVEL BACK IN TIME
Would I go back? Oh yes I would.
But I'm content with what is mine.
I don't complain, it does no good.

www.ingramcontent.com/pod-product-compliance
Lightning Source LLC
Chambersburg PA
CBHW071015120626
46546CB00003B/1096